Math in Focus®

Singapore Math®
by Marshall Cavendish

Assessment Guide

Marshall Cavendish
Education

U.S. Distributor

Houghton Mifflin Harcourt.
The Learning Company™

Grade 1

© 2020 Marshall Cavendish Education Pte Ltd

Published by Marshall Cavendish Education
Times Centre, 1 New Industrial Road, Singapore 536196
Customer Service Hotline: (65) 6213 9688
US Office Tel: (1-914) 332 8888 | Fax: (1-914) 332 8882
E-mail: cs@mceducation.com
Website: www.mceducation.com

Distributed by
Houghton Mifflin Harcourt
125 High Street
Boston, MA 02110
Tel: 617-351-5000
Website: www.hmhco.com/programs/math-in-focus

First published 2020

ISBN 978-0-358-10317-2

Printed in Singapore

1 2 3 4 5 6 7 8   1401   25 24 23 22 21 20
4500759432   A B C D E

Contents

BLANK

Preface

Welcome!

The assessments in **Math in F⊚cus**®: *Assessment Guide* accompany **Math in F⊚cus**®: *Student Edition*. Assessment resources provide your teacher with the critical information they need to evaluate your achievement, determine the need for intervention, and to shape future instruction.

Math in F⊚cus®: *Assessment Guide* includes:

- **Chapter Tests** — to help your teacher determine whether you have acquired specific skills and concepts

- **Cumulative Reviews** — to help your teacher form a larger picture of your ongoing progress

Assessments in **Math in F⊚cus**® *Assessment Guide* employ a variety of test item formats including multiple-choice, short answer questions, and constructed response.

Today, you will take a test to show what you have learned. The test has three sections: A, B, and C. You must complete all the sections within the time given by your teacher.

Directions

1.   Read each question and follow the directions.
2.   Erase your mark completely if you need to change an answer.
3.   Some questions ask you to show or explain your work to earn points.
4.   Skip questions if you do not know the answers.
5.   Review your work if you finish early.

Chapter Test

2 Assessment Guide
Addition and Subtraction Within 10

Section A   Multiple-Choice Questions

| 3 | 4 | 5 | 7 |

Three of the numbers above are used to make a number bond.
Which number is **not** used?

(A) 3

(B) 4

(C) 5

(D) 7

2 Look at the picture.
Some rabbits hop away.
How many rabbits are left?

(A) 6 − 3 = 3

(B) 6 + 3 = 9

(C) 9 − 6 = 3

(D) 9 − 3 = 6

3 6 + 2 = _____ + 1
What is the missing number?

(A) 5

(B) 7

(C) 8

(D) 9

Section B   Short Answer Questions

4 John has 4 stickers.
Ava has 5 stickers.
How many stickers do they have in all?

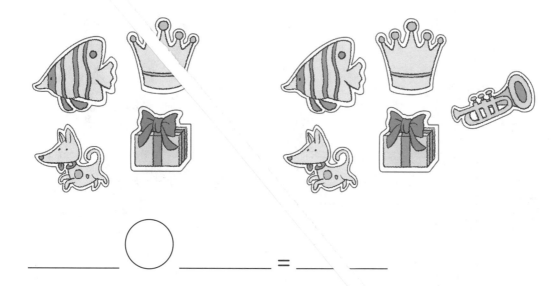

_____ ◯ _____ = ___ ___

They have _____ stickers in all.

5 There are 10 pencils.
Mariah takes some pencils.
There are 4 pencils left.
How many pencils does Mariah take?

_____ ◯ _____ = _____

Mariah takes _____ pencils.

6 Julian is solving the following problem:

$3 +$ _____ $= 7$

He writes:

+ means add.
So, I add 3 and 7 to find the missing number.

Circle Julian's mistake.
Then, find the missing number.
Draw or write to show your work.

So, $3 +$ _____ $= 7$.

Section C   Constructed Response

7 I have two numbers.
I get 10 when I add both numbers.
I get 2 when I subtract one number from the other.
What are my two numbers?

Show your work and write your answers in the blanks below.

My two numbers are _____ and _____.

Name: _____ Date: _____

Assessment Guide
Shapes and Patterns

Section A   Multiple-Choice Questions

1 Look at the picture.
What flat shape do you see?

Ⓐ circle

Ⓑ rectangle

Ⓒ square

Ⓓ triangle

2 Look at the picture.
What solid shape do you see?

Ⓐ sphere

Ⓑ rectangular prism

Ⓒ cone

Ⓓ cube

3 What solid shapes come next in the pattern?

A)

B)

C)

D)

Section B   Short Answer Questions

4 Count each flat shape in the picture.
Write each answer in the table.

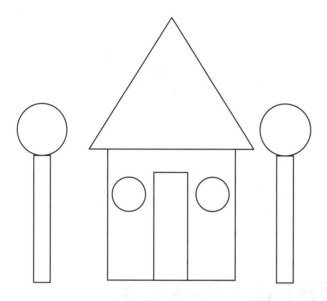

	Flat Shape	Number
a	Square	
b	Triangle	
c	Circle	
d	Rectangle	

5 Count each solid shape in the picture.
Write each answer in the table.

	Solid Shape	Number
a	Cube	
b	Cylinder	
c	Cone	
d	Sphere	

6 Jordan has two triangles.

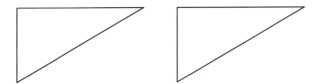

a   He says he can make a new shape with three sides.
Draw the shape he can make.

b   He says he can make a new shape with four corners.
Draw the shape he can make.

Section C   Constructed Response

7 Look at the pattern below.

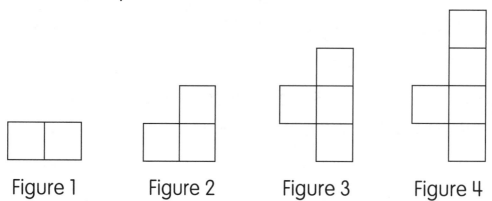

Figure 1   Figure 2   Figure 3   Figure 4

a   Draw Figure 5.

b   Which figure has 10 squares?

Show your work and write your answer in the blank below.

Figure _____ has 10 squares.

Assessment Guide
Cumulative Review 1

Section A   Multiple-Choice Questions

1 How many are there?

(A) 4

(B) 5

(C) 6

(D) 7

2 Look at the number pattern.
What are the missing numbers?

? 5 4 3 2 ?

(A) 6, 0

(B) 6, 1

(C) 7, 0

(D) 7, 1

3 Which tank has 2 fish?

(A)

(B)

(C)

(D)

4 How many triangles are there in all?

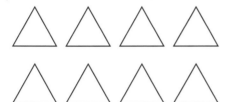 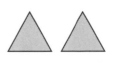

(A) 2

(B) 6

(C) 8

(D) 10

5 Look at the picture.
How many frogs are there in all?

(A) $5 - 2 = 3$

(B) $7 - 2 = 5$

(C) $5 + 2 = 7$

(D) $5 + 3 = 8$

6 Which of these is false?

(A) 4 + 5 = 9

(B) 5 − 4 = 9

(C) 9 − 4 = 5

(D) 9 − 5 = 4

7 ★ + 3 = 2 + 5

What is the value of ★?

(A) 2

(B) 4

(C) 7

(D) 10

8 How many different types of shapes do you see?

(A) 3

(B) 4

(C) 5

(D) 6

9 What flat shapes come next in the pattern?

(A) ○ ▯

(B) △ ☐

(C) ☐ ○

(D) ▯ △

10 Which flat shapes are divided into halves?

(A) circle and triangle

(B) circle and rectangle

(C) square and triangle

(D) square and rectangle

Section B Short Answer Questions

11 Which solid shape can stack, roll, and slide?

_____

12 **a** What flat shape can you make with and ?

_____

b What flat shape can you make with and ?

_____

13 Look at the picture below.

Luna writes a fact family on the picture above.

$5 + 4 = 9$	$6 + 3 = 9$
$9 - 5 = 4$	$9 - 6 = 3$

Luna makes two mistakes in her work.
Circle them.
Then, write the correct number sentences below.

_____ ◯ _____ = _____

_____ ◯ _____ = _____

14 △, ◯, and ☐ each stands for a number.

$$\triangle + \triangle = 10$$

$$\square + \bigcirc = 8$$

$$\triangle - \bigcirc = 3$$

Find the value of △, ◯, and ☐.

Show your work and write your answers in the blanks below.

△ = _____

◯ = _____

☐ = _____

Chapter Test 4 Assessment Guide
Numbers to 20

Section A Multiple-Choice Questions

1 What are the missing numbers?

_____ = _____ ten _____ ones

(A) 10, 1, 0   (B) 10, 1, 4
(C) 14, 1, 4   (D) 14, 4, 1

2 Order 15, 19, and 13 from greatest to least.

(A) 13, 15, 19   (B) 15, 19, 13
(C) 19, 13, 15   (D) 19, 15, 13

3 Isaac can make a number pattern with his number cards.
Two of the cards are covered up.
Which of the following **cannot** be the two numbers?

(A) 17, 19   (B) 7, 9
(C) 10, 12   (D) 12, 14

Section B Short Answer Questions

4 Compare the numbers.
Write the answer in each blank.

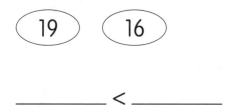

_____ < _____

5 Look at the pattern.
Then, fill in each blank.

_____ , _____ , 16 , 14 , 12 , 10 , 8

6 Ethan is solving the following problem:

Fill in the circle with **<**, **>**, or **=**.

1 ten 3 ones ◯ 13 ones

He writes:

There is 1 ten in 1 ten 3 ones.

There are no tens in 13 ones.

1 ten is greater than 0 tens.

So, 1 ten 3 ones > 13 ones.

Circle where Ethan first made a mistake.
Then, draw or write to show how you would compare
1 ten 3 ones and 13 ones.

1 ten 3 ones ◯ 13 ones

Section C Constructed Response

7 Alyssa wants to know which number is greatest, 12, 15, or 9.
Logan says that 9 ones are greater than 2 ones and 5 ones.
So, 9 is the greatest.

a Write down Logan's mistake.

_____

_____.

Then, show how you would find the greatest number.

Show your work and write your answer in the blank below.

The greatest number is _____.

b Order the numbers from greatest to least.

_____, _____, _____
   greatest   least

Chapter Test

5

Assessment Guide
Addition and
Subtraction Within 20

Section A   Multiple-Choice Questions

1 Look at the picture.
What is the correct doubles fact?

(A) $3 + 3 = 6$

(B) $4 + 4 = 8$

(C) $5 + 5 = 10$

(D) $6 + 6 = 12$

2 Which of the following does **not** have the same value
as $8 + 4$?

(A) $7 + 5$

(B) $13 - 1$

(C) $14 - 3$

(D) $4 + 8$

3 ★ and ✳ each stands for a number.

$$12 - ★ = 8$$
$$✳ - ★ = 7$$

Find the value of ✳.

(A) 3

(B) 4

(C) 11

(D) 13

Section B   Short Answer Questions

4 Camila writes the following.

> Doubles 6 is 1 more than doubles 5 because 6 is 1 more than 5.

What is Camila's mistake?
Fill in each blank to find out.

Doubles 6 = _____ $\bigcirc$ _____ = _____

Doubles 5 = _____ $\bigcirc$ _____ = _____

_____ $\bigcirc$ _____ = _____

Doubles 6 is _____ than doubles 5.

5 David has 8 stamps.
Isabel has 5 stamps.
How many stamps do they have in all?

_____ ◯ _____ = _____

They have _____ stamps in all.

6 Zoey has 12 books.
She gives Luke some books.
She has 3 books left.
How many books does Zoey give Luke?

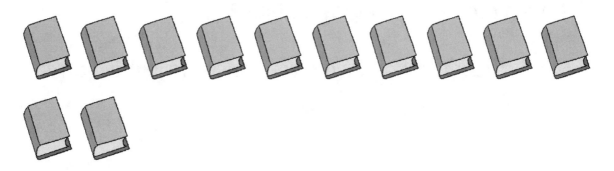

_____ ◯ _____ = _____

Zoey gives Luke _____ books.

Section C   Constructed Response

7 Tyler is reading a book.
The page numbers of the two pages Tyler is looking at adds up to 17.
What are the two page numbers?

Show your work and write your answers in the blanks below.

The two page numbers are _____ and _____.

Assessment Guide
Cumulative Review 2

Section A   Multiple-Choice Questions

1 What are the missing numbers?

_____ = _____ ten _____ ones

(A) 15, 1, 5

(B) 15, 5, 1

(C) 16, 1, 6

(D) 16, 6, 1

2 What are the numbers from least to greatest?

(A) 19, 14, 11

(B) 14, 11, 19

(C) 11, 19, 14

(D) 11, 14, 19

3 Look at the number pattern.
What are the missing numbers?

(A) 20, 17

(B) 20, 18

(C) 21, 17

(D) 21, 18

4 Compare the numbers.
Which of these is true?

11   18   13

(A) 11 is greater than 13.

(B) 13 is the greatest number.

(C) 18 is greater than 11.

(D) 18 is the least number.

5 Look at the number pattern.
What are the missing numbers?

(A) 9, 10

(B) 10, 11

(C) 10, 12

(D) 11, 12

6 Andrea has 16 apples.
9 apples are red.
The rest are green.
How many apples are green?

(A) 7

(B) 8

(C) 9

(D) 16

7 Find the missing number.
Use the counting tape to help you.

12 + _____ = 16

| 12 | 13 | 14 | 15 | 16 | 17 | 18 |

(A) 2

(B) 3

(C) 4

(D) 5

8 Joseph has 9 roses.
Michelle gives him 8 more roses.
How many roses does Joseph have in all?

(A) 8

(B) 9

(C) 17

(D) 18

9 △ and ⬡ each stands for a number.

△ + △ = 12

△ + ⬡ = 14

Find the value of ⬡.

(A) 6

(B) 8

(C) 12

(D) 20

10 Alan has 13 pencils.
Mia has 17 pencils.
Which of these is true?

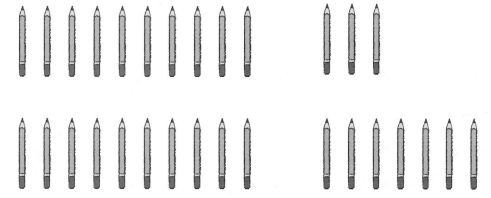

(A) Mia has 3 more pencils than Alan.

(B) Mia has 4 more pencils than Alan.

(C) Alan has 3 more pencils than Mia.

(D) Alan has 4 more pencils than Mia.

Section B Short Answer Questions

11 Write each number in word.

a 19 _____

b 15 _____

12 Aki is solving the following problem:

> Find the number that makes the number sentence true.
>
> 8 + 9 = _____ − 3

He writes:

> 8 + 9 = 17
> So, 17 − 3 = 14
> The missing number is 14.

Circle Aki's mistake.
Then, show how you would find the missing number.

So, 8 + 9 = _____ − 3.

13 Andrew and Faith need to bake 16 pies in all for charity.
Andrew bakes 9 pies.
Faith bakes 6 pies.
Did they manage to bake 16 pies in all?
Write a number sentence to show your work.
Then, circle the correct answer.

_____ $\bigcirc$ _____ = _____

They   managed   /   did not manage   to bake 16 pies.

Section C Constructed Response

14 Emily is 2 years older than Henry.
Both their ages add up to 18 years.
How old are Emily and Henry?

Show your work and write your answers in the blanks below.

Emily is _____ years old.

Henry is _____ years old.

Chapter Test 6
Assessment Guide
Numbers to 40

Section A Multiple-Choice Questions

1 How many  are there?

🍀🍀🍀🍀🍀🍀🍀🍀🍀🍀
🍀🍀🍀🍀🍀🍀🍀🍀🍀🍀
🍀🍀🍀🍀🍀

(A) 35

(B) 30

(C) 25

(D) 20

2 Look at the number pattern.
What are the missing numbers?

30, 31, _____, 33, 34, 35, _____, 37, 38, _____, 40

(A) 31, 36, 38

(B) 32, 36, 38

(C) 32, 36, 39

(D) 33, 36, 39

3 Which of the following does **not** show the number of  ?

Ⓐ 3 tens 0 ones

Ⓑ 2 tens 10 ones

Ⓒ 20 tens 10 ones

Ⓓ 0 tens 30 ones

Section B   Short Answer Questions

4 Compare the numbers.
Write the answer in each blank.

    a   The least number is _____.

    b   The greatest number is _____.

5 Write all the numbers less than 40 but greater than 36.

_____

6 Sarah writes the following:

> 37 is greater than 33.
>
> 4 less than 33 is 37.

Circle Sarah's mistake.
Then, write the correct sentence below.

_____

Section C   Constructed Response

7 A, B, and C each stands for a different number.

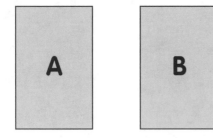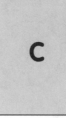

A is 2 less than 4 tens.
B is 3 less than A.
C is greater than B.
A is the greatest number.
What numbers can C be?

Show your work and write your answers in the blanks below.

C can be _____ or _____.

Chapter Test 7

Assessment Guide
Calendar and Time

Section A   Multiple-Choice Questions

1 Look at the calendar.
What day of the week is April 18?

April						
Sun.	Mon.	Tue.	Wed.	Thu.	Fri.	Sat.
	1	2	3	4	5	6
7	8	9	10	11	12	13
14	15	16	17	18	19	20
21	22	23	24	25	26	27
28	29	30				

(A) Sunday

(B) Wednesday

(C) Thursday

(D) Saturday

2 Look at the clock.
What is the time?

(A) 5:00

(B) 6:00

(C) 7:00

(D) 12:00

3 The clock shows the time an hour after Carla goes to bed.
What time does Carla go to bed?

(A) half past 9

(B) half past 8

(C) half past 7

(D) half past 6

Section B   Short Answer Questions

4 Write the days of the week in order.

_____, _____, Tuesday,

_____, _____, _____,

_____

5 Write all the months with 31 days.

The months are _____, _____,

_____, _____, _____, _____,

and _____.

6 Trevon shows the time half past 8.

Circle what is wrong with Trevon's clock.
Then, draw the clock hands to show half past 8.

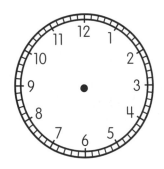

Section C   Constructed Response

7 Look at the calendar below.

August						
Sun.	**Mon.**	**Tue.**	**Wed.**	**Thu.**	**Fri.**	**Sat.**
	1	2	3	4	5	6
7	8	9	10	11	12	13
14	15	16	17	18	19	20
21	22	23	24	25	26	27
28	29	30	31			

a   What is the date of the last day of the month?

The date is _____.

b   What is the date a week after the last day of August?

Show your work and write your answer in the blank below.

The date a week after the last day of August

is _____.

Assessment Guide
Cumulative Review 3

Section A Multiple-Choice Questions

1. How many 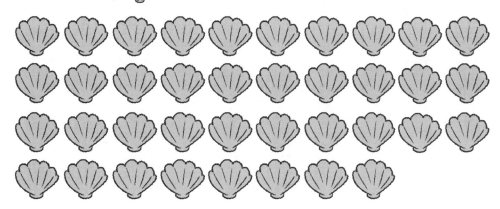 are there?

(A) 28

(B) 36

(C) 38

(D) 40

2. Compare the numbers.

23   32

Which of these is false?

(A) 23 < 32

(B) 23 is less than 32.

(C) 32 < 23

(D) 32 is greater than 23.

3 Count on by tens and ones.
What are the missing numbers?

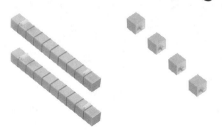

_____ = _____ tens _____ ones

- (A) 20, 2, 0
- (B) 24, 2, 4
- (C) 24, 4, 2
- (D) 34, 3, 4

4 Parker has 27 beads.
Emma has 32 beads.
Shanti has 34 beads.
Which of the following is true?

- (A) Emma has more beads than Parker.
- (B) Emma has the most beads.
- (C) Shanti has the fewest beads.
- (D) Parker has more beads than Shanti.

5 Look at the number pattern.
What are the missing numbers?

- **A** 30, 29
- **B** 30, 28
- **C** 29, 28
- **D** 29, 25

6 What day is three days before Wednesday?
- **A** Tuesday
- **B** Thursday
- **C** Saturday
- **D** Sunday

7 What date is it three weeks from August 17?
- **A** August 20
- **B** August 31
- **C** September 7
- **D** September 17

8 Look at the digital clock.

Which clock shows the same time?

(A)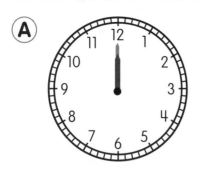

(B)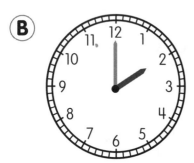

(C)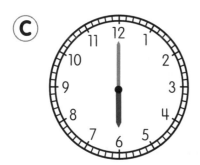

(D)

9 The minute hand of a clock points at 12.
The hour hand points at 6.
What is the time shown?

(A) 12 o'clock

(B) 6 o'clock

(C) half past 12

(D) half past 6

10 What is an hour after the time shown?

(A) 2 o'clock

(B) half past 2

(C) half past 3

(D) 4 o'clock

Section B   Short Answer Questions

11 Look at the picture below.

How many rabbits are there?
Make groups of 10.
Then, count on and fill in each blank.

Tens	Ones

12 These number cards make a number pattern.
Find the missing numbers.
Write the answer in each blank.

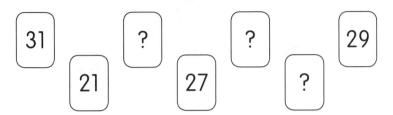

31   ?   ?   29

    21   27   ?

The missing numbers are _____ , _____ , and

_____ .

13 Miranda and Wyatt describe the positions of the clock
hands at half past 9.

The minute hand points at 6.
The hour hand points
between 8 and 9.

The minute hand points at 6.
The hour hand points
between 9 and 10.

Miranda   Wyatt

Draw clock hands to show who is correct.
Then, circle the name.

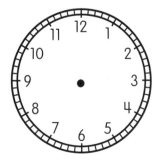

Miranda   /   Wyatt   is correct.

Section C Constructed Response

14 Look at the torn calendar below.

May						
Sun.	Mon.	Tue.	Wed.	Thu.	Fri.	Sat.
1	2	3	4	5	6	
8	9	10	11			
15	16	17				
22	23					
29						

a What is the date of the third Saturday?

Show your work and write your answer in the blank below.

The date is _____.

b What is the date two weeks after the third Saturday of May?

Show your work and write your answers in the blanks below.

The date is _____.

Chapter Test 8

Assessment Guide
Addition and
Subtraction Within 40

Section A   Multiple-Choice Questions

1 Add.
Use the counting tape to help you.
What is the missing number?

$21 + 5 =$ _____

| 21 | 22 | 23 | 24 | 25 | 26 | 27 |

Ⓐ 24

Ⓑ 25

Ⓒ 26

Ⓓ 27

2 Add.
What is the missing number?

Tens Ones

```
      2   3
  +       9
  _____
      ?
```

Ⓐ 29

Ⓑ 31

Ⓒ 32

Ⓓ 33

3 Subtract.
What is the missing number?

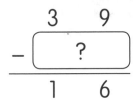

	Tens	Ones
	3	9
−	?	
	1	6

(A) 33

(B) 23

(C) 13

(D) 3

Section B   Short Answer Questions

4 Alex has 6 toy cars.
Jess has 5 toy cars.
Clara has 8 toy cars.
How many toy cars do the three children have in all?

The three children have _____ toy cars in all.

5 Look at the picture.
Write the answer in each blank.

a   5 + 5 + 5 = _____

b   3 fives = _____

6 Vicente is solving the following problem:

33 − 18 = _____

He writes:

> − means subtract.
>
> So, I subtract the digit that is less from the greater digit in each place.
>
> | Tens | Ones |
> |:---:|:---:|
> | 3 | 3 |
> | − 1 | 8 |
> | 2 | 5 |

Circle all of Vicente's mistake.
Then, write to show how you use place value to subtract.

So, 33 − 18 = _____.

Section C   Constructed Response

7 Carrie, Hugo, and Zane fold some paper stars.
Carrie folds 5 more stars than Zane.
Zane folds 6 more stars than Hugo.

a _____ folds the greatest number of stars.

b How many more stars does Carrie fold than Hugo?

Show your work and write your answer in the blank below.

Carrie folds _____ more stars than Hugo.

Chapter Test 9

Assessment Guide
Length and Weight

Section A   Multiple-Choice Questions

1 Which row of  is the longest?

Ⓐ

Ⓑ

Ⓒ

Ⓓ

2 Each ▭ stands for 1 unit.
How many units long is the scarf?

Ⓐ about 10 units long

Ⓑ about 9 units long

Ⓒ about 8 units long

Ⓓ about 7 units long

3 Each 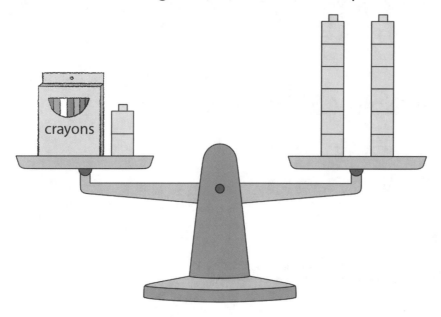 stands for 1 unit.
What is the weight of the box of crayons?

A about 8 units

B about 10 units

C about 12 units

D about 14 units

Section B Short Answer Questions

4 Look at the picture.
Write the answer in each blank.

Crayon A

Crayon B

Crayon C

a Crayon _____ is the longest.

b Crayon _____ is the shortest.

5 Look at the picture.
Write **apple** or **pear** in each blank.

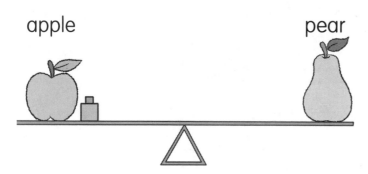

apple   pear

a   The _____ is lighter than the _____.

b   The _____ is heavier than the _____.

6 Look at the picture below.

Each  stands for 1 unit.

Eduardo writes the following sentence:

> The girl is 1 unit taller than the boy.

What is Eduardo's mistake?
Fill in each blank to find out.
Then, help Eduardo correct his sentence.

Height of the boy = _____ units

Height of the girl = _____ units

_____ ◯ _____ = _____

Correct sentence: _____

Section C   Constructed Response

7 Look at the picture below.

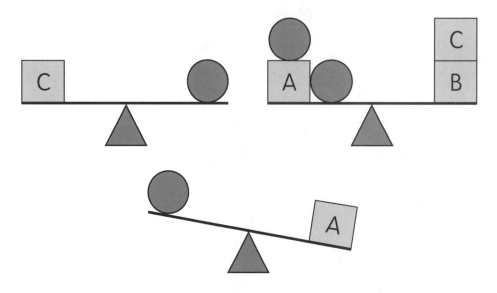

a Which is heavier, Box A or Box C?

Box _____ is heavier.

b Box _____ is the lightest box

c Box _____ is the heaviest box.

Assessment Guide
Numbers to 120

Section A Multiple-Choice Questions

1 How many 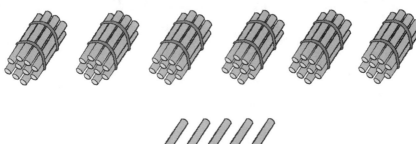 are there?

(A) 55

(B) 50

(C) 65

(D) 75

2 Which of the following is **not** equal to 88?

(A) 8 tens 8 ones

(B) 7 tens 18 ones

(C) 4 tens 38 ones

(D) 3 tens 58 ones

3 P, Q, and R each stands for a number.
P > Q
P < R
What numbers can P, Q, and R be?

(A) P = 65, Q = 58, R = 63

(B) P = 73, Q = 78, R = 75

(C) P = 53, Q = 48, R = 46

(D) P = 65, Q = 58, R = 69

Section B   Short Answer Questions

4 Write each number in word.

a 57 _____

b 112 _____

5 Write each missing number

	Tens	Ones			Tens	Ones
91 =	8		=			31

6 Look at the numbers below.

69   73   63

Jasmine wants to find the greatest number.
She writes:

> First, I compare the ones.
> 9 ones are greater than 3 ones.
> So, 69 is the greatest.

What is Jasmine's mistake?

_____

Write how you would use place value to find the greatest number.

The greatest number is _____.

Section C   Constructed Response

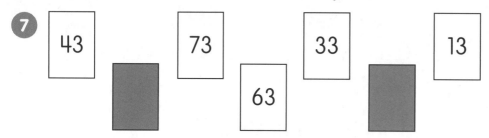

There are seven number cards.
These number cards make a pattern.

a   What are the two missing numbers?

The two missing numbers are _____
and _____.

b   Make a number pattern with all the numbers.

My number pattern is _____, _____, _____,

_____, _____, _____, _____.

Describe your number pattern.

_____

_____

Assessment Guide
Cumulative Review 4

Section A   Multiple-Choice Questions

1 What is the weight of the doll?

A about 12 🫘
B about 10 🫘
C about 11 🫘
D about 9 🫘

2 Which of these is true?

Flower A

Flower B

Flower C

(A) Flower A is longer than Flower B.

(B) Flower B is longer than Flower A.

(C) Flower C is longer than Flower A.

(D) Flower C is longer than Flower B.

3 How long is the ribbon?

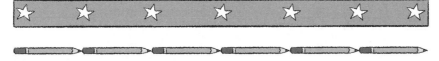

(A) about 5 long

(B) about 6 long

(C) about 7 long

(D) about 8 ⟶ long

4 What are the numbers from least to greatest?

{ 95 }   { 85 }   { 87 }

(A) 85, 87, 95

(B) 85, 95, 87

(C) 87, 95, 85

(D) 95, 87, 85

5 What is the missing number?

93 = _____ tens 23 ones

Ⓐ 9

Ⓑ 8

Ⓒ 7

Ⓓ 6

6 Compare the numbers.
Which of these is true?

  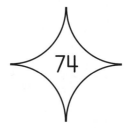

Ⓐ 67 is greater than 76.

Ⓑ 67 is less than 74.

Ⓒ 67 is the greatest.

Ⓓ 67 is the same as 76.

7 Subtract.
What is the missing number?

Tens Ones

```
   3    4
−  [ ? ]
───────────
   2    8
```

(A) 4

(B) 6

(C) 14

(D) 16

8 🌸 and 🍃 each stands for a number.

🌸 + 🌸 + 🌸 = 18

🌸 + 🍃 = 25

What is the value of ?

(A) 7

(B) 19

(C) 22

(D) 31

9 Luis has 4 crayons at first.
His sister gives him 6 crayons.
His brother gives him 3 crayons.
How many crayons does Luis have in all?

(A) 10

(B) 12

(C) 13

(D) 14

10 Kayla saw 32 animals at a zoo.
Dae saw 6 more animals than Kayla.
How many animals did Dae see?

(A) 26

(B) 28

(C) 36

(D) 38

Section B   Short Answer Questions

11 Each 🪣 stands for 1 unit.

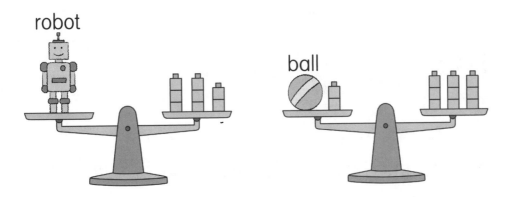

The robot is 1 unit lighter than the ball.

Dylan

What is Dylan's mistake?
Fill in each blank to find out.
Then, help Dylan correct his sentence.

Weight of the robot = _____ units

Weight of the ball = _____ units

_____ ◯ _____ = _____

Correct sentence: _____

12 Look at the picture below.

Juan and Alexa use different ways to describe the number of flowers.

Juan writes: | Doubles 6 |

Alexa writes: | 6 twos |

Show that both of their ways are correct.
Use the picture to help you.

Juan's way:

There are _____ rows of 6.

_____ ◯ _____ = _____

Alexa's way:

There are _____ groups of 2.

_____ ◯ _____ ◯ _____ ◯ _____

_____ ◯ _____ ◯ _____ = _____

13 Thomas solves 19 math questions.
He solves 4 fewer questions than Constance.
How many questions does Constance solve?

Constance solves _____ questions.

Section C   Constructed Response

14 Look at the picture below.
Each ● stands for 1 unit.

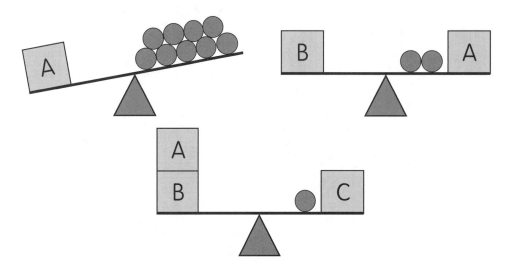

One more ● is needed to balance Box A.
What are the weights of Boxes A, B, and C?

Show your work and write your answers in the blanks below.

Box A = _____ units

Box B = _____ units

Box C = _____ units

Chapter Test 11

Assessment Guide
Addition and
Subtraction Within 100

Section A   Multiple-Choice Questions

1 Add.
What is the missing number?

Tens	Ones
2	2
+ 3	4

   [?]

Ⓐ 46

Ⓑ 50

Ⓒ 56

Ⓓ 66

2 Add.
What are the missing numbers?

Tens	Ones
[X]	9
+ 2	[Y]
8	5

Ⓐ X = 6, Y = 4   Ⓑ X = 6, Y = 6

Ⓒ X = 5, Y = 4   Ⓓ X = 5, Y = 6

3 Find the missing number.

Tens Ones

$$
\begin{array}{r}
8 \quad 5 \\
- \; \boxed{\quad ? \quad} \\
\hline
6 \quad 7
\end{array}
$$

(**A**) 12

(**B**) 18

(**C**) 22

(**D**) 28

Section B   Short Answer Questions

4 Find each missing number.

a

Tens	Ones
7	2
+ 1	6

☐

b

Tens	Ones
8	5
− 3	3

☐

5 Solve.
Write the answer in each blank.

a $76 + \underline{\hspace{2cm}} = 86$

b $\underline{\hspace{2cm}} - 10 = 83$

6 Hailey wants to subtract 9 from 53.
She shows her work this way:

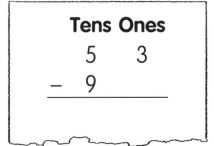

9 cannot be subtracted from 5.
So, 9 cannot be subtracted from 53.

Hailey

Circle the mistake in Hailey's work.
Then, show Hailey how to subtract 9 from 53 correctly.
Show your work in the space below.

Section C   Constructed Response

7 Look at the pattern below.

 and  each stands for a number.

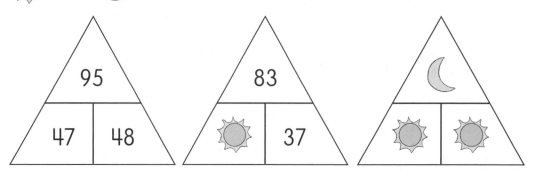

Find the value of ☀ and ☾.

Show your work and write your answers in the blanks below.

☀ = _____   ☾ = _____

Chapter Test 12

Assessment Guide
Graphs

Section A   Multiple-Choice Questions

1 Look at the picture graph.
   The graph shows how many pieces of fruit Ms. Smith bought.

Fruit Ms. Smith Bought

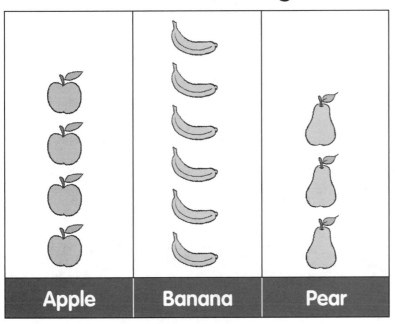

How many pieces of fruit did Ms. Smith buy?

(A) 3

(B) 4

(C) 6

(D) 13

2 Look at the tally chart.
The tally chart shows the different types of vegetables
Mr. Brown bought.

Type of Vegetables	Tally	Number
Carrot	⫿⫿⫿⫿	5
Potato	?	?
Tomato	‖	2

Mr. Brown bought the same number of pototoes
as carrots.
How many potatoes and tomatoes did Mr. Brown buy?

(A) 10

(B) 7

(C) 5

(D) 4

3 Look at the picture graph.
The graph shows the favorite playground activities
of some children.

Our Favorite Playground Activities

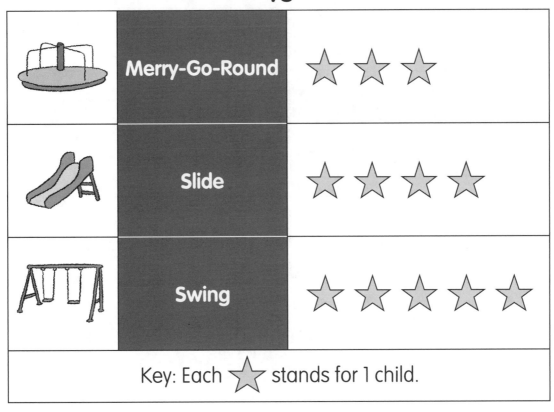

How many children like to play on the slide or the swing?

(A) 4

(B) 5

(C) 7

(D) 9

Section B   Short Answer Questions

4 Some children visited a forest.
They made a tally chart to show the number of animals they saw in the forest.

a   Count the tally marks for each type of animal.
Then, write each answer in the table.

Type of Animals	Tally	Number
Deer	ⅢⅡ	
Rabbit	ⅠⅠⅠⅠ	
Squirrel	ⅢⅢ ⅠⅠⅠⅠ	

b   They saw _____ more squirrels than deer.

5 Ms. Lee had her students vote for their favorite colors. The number of students who voted for green is shown in the picture graph.

Our Favorite Colors

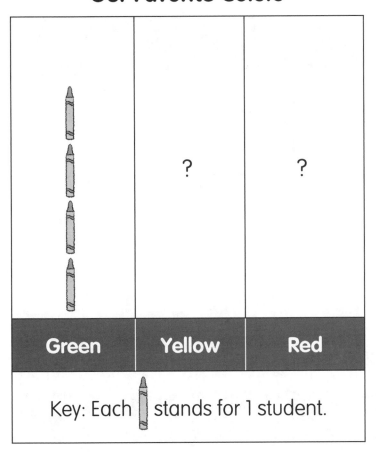

Key: Each ✎ stands for 1 student.

a The same number of students voted for yellow as green.

_____ students voted for yellow.

b Most students voted for red.
What is the least number of students who voted

for red? _____.

6 25 students are asked to choose their favorite sport.
10 students like baseball.
3 more students like basketball than football.
Kate makes a tally chart to show the information.

Type of Sport	Tally	Number
Basketball	卌 ‖	6
Baseball	卌 ‖‖	10
Football	卌 ‖‖	9

What are Kate's mistakes?
Circle them.

Then, make the correct tally chart.

Type of Sport	Tally	Number
Basketball		
Baseball		
Football		

Section C   Constructed Response

7 Look at the picture graph.
The picture graph shows the favorite flowers of some children.

Favorite Flowers

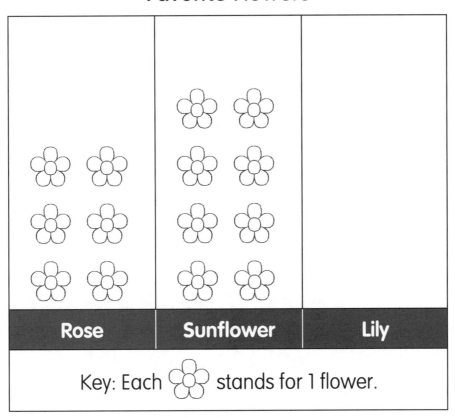

Key: Each 🌼 stands for 1 flower.

a 3 more children like lilies than sunflowers.

Draw 🌼 to show the number.

b How many children are there in all?

Show your work and write your answer in the blank below.

There are _____ children in all.

BLANK

13

Assessment Guide
Money

Section A   Multiple-Choice Questions

1 How many dimes are there?

(A) 3

(B) 4

(C) 5

(D) 8

2 Which set can you exchange for a dime?

(A) [penny, penny]

(B) [nickel, nickel]

(C) [dime, dime]

(D) [nickel, nickel, nickel, nickel, nickel]

3 Daniel has four coins.
The total value of his coins is 65¢.
What are the coins he has?

(A) 1 quarter, 2 dimes, 1 nickel

(B) 1 quarter, 3 dimes

(C) 2 quarters, 1 dime, 1 nickel

(D) 2 quarters, 2 nickels

Section B   Short Answer Questions

4 Count.
Write the answer in each blank.

a   The value of the coins is _____¢ in all.

b   I can make _____ quarters with these coins.

5 An exercise book costs 35¢.
Adam has 3 quarters.
He is not sure if he has enough money to buy two books.
Does Adam have enough money?

Fill in each blank to find out.
Then, circle the correct answer.

_____¢ ◯ _____¢ = _____¢

The two exercise books cost _____¢.

3 quarters = _____¢

Adam   has   /   does not have   enough money.

6 These are some items on sale.
Write the answer in each blank.

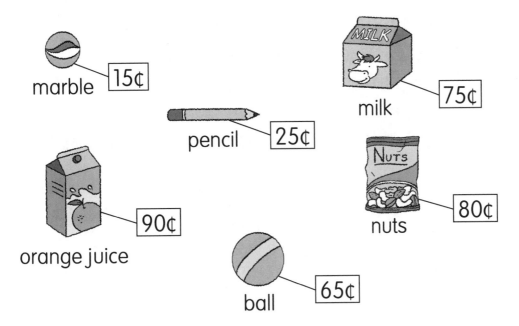

marble 15¢

pencil 25¢

milk 75¢

orange juice 90¢

nuts 80¢

ball 65¢

a Anna has 80¢.
She wants to buy something to drink.

She can buy a carton of _____ to drink.

b Owen has 85¢.
After buying something, he has 70¢ left.

He buys a _____.

Section C   Constructed Response

7 Claire has 90¢.
She uses all her money to buy a ruler and a pencil.
The ruler costs 20¢ more than the pencil.
How much does the ruler cost?

Show your work and write your answer in the blank below.

The ruler costs _____¢.

Assessment Guide
Cumulative Review 5

Section A Multiple-Choice Questions

1 Add.
What is the missing number?

$78 + 7 =$ _____

(A) 83

(B) 84

(C) 85

(D) 87

2 Add.
What is the missing number?

Tens	Ones
4	3
+ ?	
6	8

(A) 5

(B) 20

(C) 25

(D) 52

3 Subtract.
What is the missing number?

81 – 50 = _____

  (A) 41

  (B) 30

  (C) 31

  (D) 21

4 Subtract.
What is the missing number?

Tens Ones

$$
\begin{array}{cc}
9 & 2 \\
- \boxed{\quad ? \quad} \\
\hline
6 & 9 \\
\end{array}
$$

  (A) 23

  (B) 27

  (C) 33

  (D) 37

5 Look at the picture graph.
The graph shows the number of birds Mr. Lopez saw
in a park.

Birds Mr. Lopez Saw

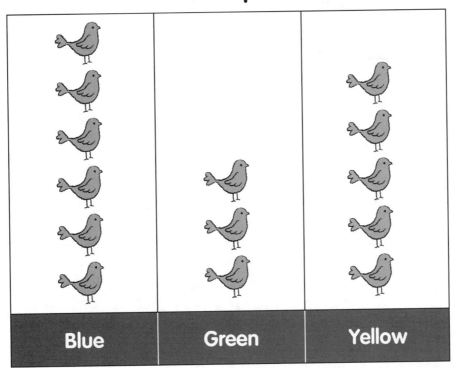

How many birds did Mr. Lopez see in all?

(A) 15

(B) 14

(C) 11

(D) 8

6 Look at the tally chart.
The chart shows the favorite books of some children.

Type of Books	Tally
History	||
Math	‖‖ |
Science	||||

How many children like Math or Science books?

(A) 6

(B) 8

(C) 9

(D) 10

7 Look at the picture graph.
The graph shows the favorite sport of some children.

Our Favorite Sports

Basketball	◇ ◇ ◇ ◇ ◇ ◇
Football	◇ ◇ ◇ ◇ ◇ ◇ ◇
Swimming	◇ ◇ ◇ ◇

Key: Each ◇ stands for 1 child.

How many children like swimming or football?

(A) 4

(B) 6

(C) 10

(D) 11

8 Henry buys a bookmark for 35¢ and gets   change.
How much does he have at first?

(A) 55¢

(B) 50¢

(C) 45¢

(D) 20¢

9 Which set can you exchange for a quarter?

10 How many nickels can you exchange for 2 quarters?

(A) 2

(B) 5

(C) 10

(D) 50

Section B Short Answer Questions

11 Eva saw some animals at the zoo.

a Complete the tally chart.

Type of Animals	Tally	Number
🐻 Bear		
🐘 Elephant		
🦒 Giraffe		

b Eva saw _____ animals in all.

Ryan is solving the following problem:

■ and ▲ each stands for a number.

■ $\xrightarrow{\;+\,17\;}$ ▲ $\xrightarrow{\;-\,23\;}$ 58

Find the value of ■.

He writes:

$$58 - 23 = 35$$
$$35 + 17 = 52$$

Circle Ryan's mistakes.

Then, fill in each blank to show how you find the

value of .

▲ = _____ ◯ _____ = _____

 = _____ _____ = _____

13 Grace buys a bottle of water.
The bottle of water costs 58¢.
She gives the cashier 3 quarters.
The cashier returns her 1 dime, 1 nickel, and 1 penny.
Grace says the cashier returns her 1 penny less.
Do you agree with Grace?
Fill in each blank to find out.

3 quarters = _____¢

How much change
should I receive?

Grace

_____¢ ◯ _____¢ = _____¢

How much change
did I receive?

1 dime, 1 nickel, 1 penny = _____¢

_____¢ ◯ _____¢ = _____¢

The cashier gives Grace _____.

Section C Constructed Response

14 Lucas has 100¢.
He spends all his money on 7 pencils and erasers.
A pencil costs 20¢.
An eraser costs 10¢.
How many pencils and how many erasers does
Lucas buy?

Show your work and write your answers in the blanks
below.

Lucas buys _____ pencils and _____ erasers.